I0815630

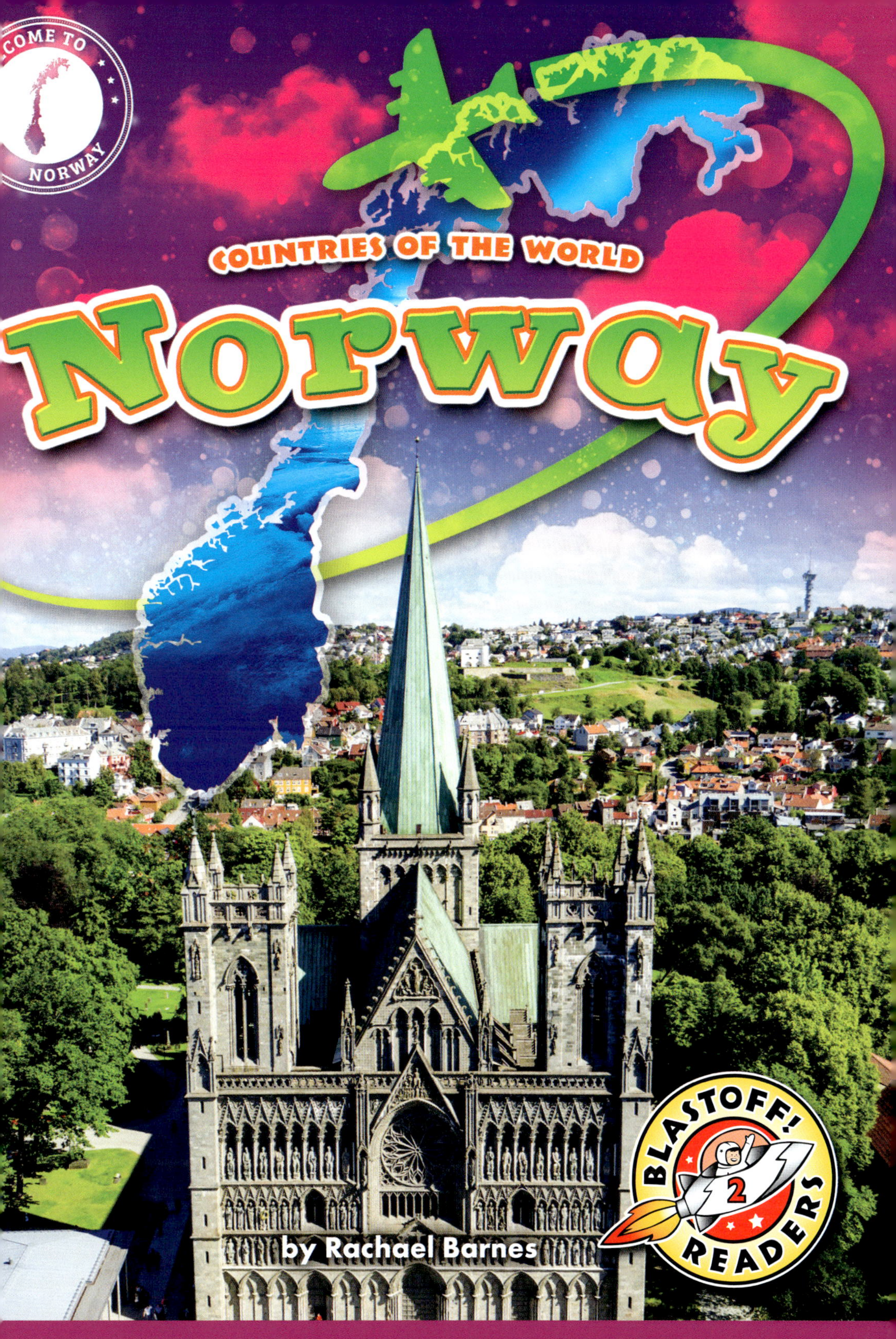

BLASTOFF! READERS, AN IMPRINT OF BELLWETHER MEDIA BY FLUTTERBEE

Blastoff! Readers are carefully developed by literacy experts to build reading stamina and move students toward fluency by combining standards-based content with developmentally appropriate text.

Level 1 provides the most support through repetition of high-frequency words, light text, predictable sentence patterns, and strong visual support.

Level 2 offers early readers a bit more challenge through varied sentences, increased text load, and text-supportive special features.

Level 3 advances early-fluent readers toward fluency through increased text load, less reliance on photos, advancing concepts, longer sentences, and more complex special features.

★ **Blastoff! Universe**

Reading Level

Grade K

Grades 1–3

Grade 4

This edition first published in 2026 by Bellwether Media, Inc.

Library of Congress Cataloging-in-Publication Data is available at www.loc.gov or upon request from the publisher.

ISBN: 9798893047868 (hardcover)
ISBN: 9798893048865 (ebook)

Editor: Ashley Kuehl Designer: Brittany McIntosh

Printed in the United States of America, North Mankato, MN.

Table of Contents

All About Norway

Norway is a country in Europe.
It is part of **Scandinavia**.
Oslo is Norway's capital.

Oceans surround much of Norway. Many islands line the coast.

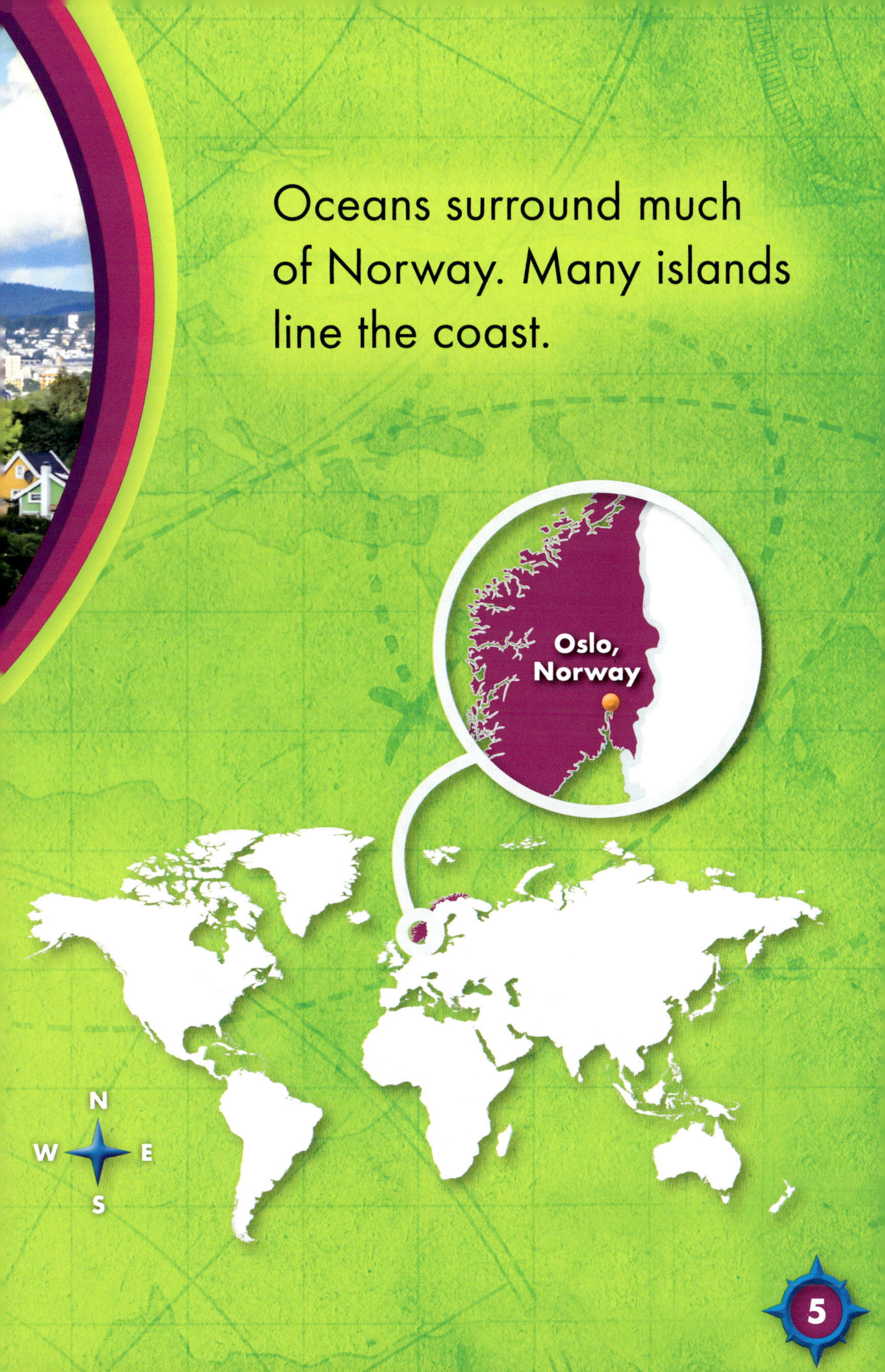

Land and Animals

Most of Norway has mountains. Snow and forests cover them.

Many rivers flow from **glaciers**. Some form waterfalls! **Fjords** cut into the coastline.

Jostedalsbreen
Size: 183 square miles (474 square kilometers)
Famous For: largest glacier in Norway

About half of Norway is in the **Arctic Circle**. Summer brings a lot of sunlight.

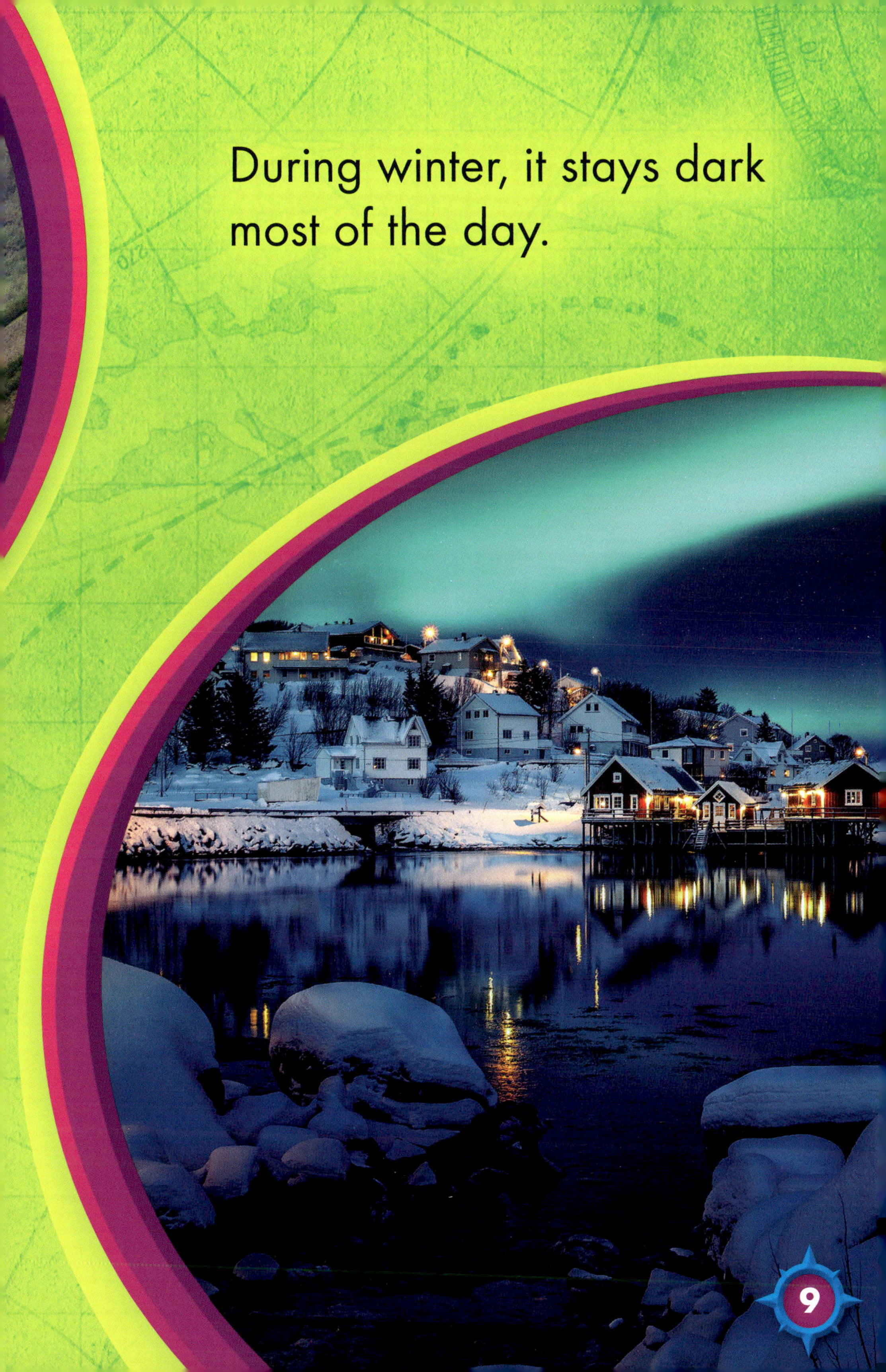

During winter, it stays dark most of the day.

White-tailed eagles fly over fjords. They hunt salmon and other fish. Whales swim along the coast.

Eurasian lynx

Animals of Norway

white-tailed eagle

Atlantic salmon

humpback whale

reindeer

Lynx live in mountain forests. Reindeer munch on mountain plants.

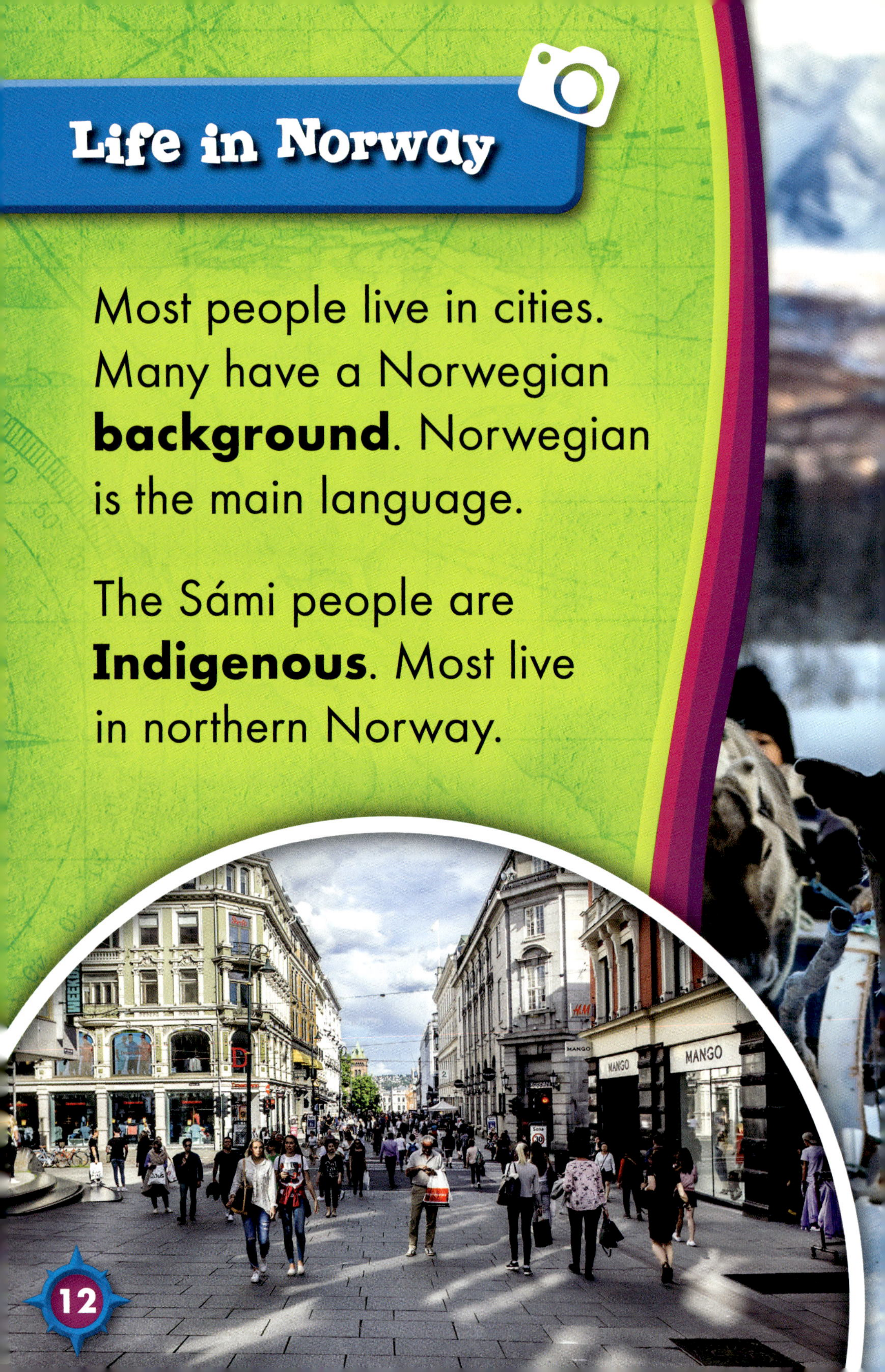

Life in Norway

Most people live in cities. Many have a Norwegian **background**. Norwegian is the main language.

The Sámi people are **Indigenous**. Most live in northern Norway.

English: Hello
Norwegian: Hei
(hi)

Most Norwegians enjoy the outdoors. Skiing and hiking are popular. Families take trips to mountain or seaside cabins.

Folk music and dancing are valued **traditions**.

Waffles and *lefse* are Norwegian favorites. Many people add *brunost* to these snacks.

Open-faced sandwiches are popular meals. *Rømmegrøt* is often made for summer **celebrations**!

May 17 is Constitution Day. Parades fill the streets. People wear *bunads* and wave Norwegian flags.

Sámi National Day is on February 6. Many celebrate the Sámi people and their **culture**!

Norway Facts

Size:
125,021 square miles
(323,802 square kilometers)

Population:
5,509,733 (2024)

National Holiday:
Constitution Day (May 17)

Main Language:
Norwegian

Capital City:
Oslo

Famous Face

Name: Aurora

Famous For: popular Norwegian singer and songwriter

Religions

Muslim: 3%

other: 29%

Lutheran: 68%

Top Landmarks

Bryggen

Oslo Opera House

Vøringsfossen Waterfall

Glossary

Arctic Circle—an imaginary line that circles the top of the globe, parallel to the equator

background—a person's experiences, knowledge, and family history

celebrations—special or fun activities for events, occasions, or holidays

culture—the beliefs, arts, and ways of life in a place or society

fjords—narrow inlets from the sea between cliffs or steep slopes

folk music—the traditional music of the people in a country or region

glaciers—massive sheets of ice that cover large areas of land

Indigenous—related to people originally from an area

Scandinavia—a region of northern Europe that includes Sweden, Denmark, and Norway

traditions—customs, ideas, or beliefs handed down from one generation to the next

To Learn More

AT THE LIBRARY

DK. *Norway*. New York, N.Y.: DK Learning, 2025.

Langdo, Bryan. *Iceland*. Minneapolis, Minn.: Bellwether Media, 2026.

Spanier, Kristine. *Norway*. Minneapolis, Minn.: Jump!, 2022.

ON THE WEB

FACTSURFER

Factsurfer.com gives you a safe, fun way to find more information.

1. Go to www.factsurfer.com.
2. Enter "Norway" into the search box and click 🔍.
3. Select your book cover to see a list of related content.

Index

The images in this book are reproduced through the courtesy of: saiko3p, front cover; Kersti Lindstrom, p. 3; Damien VERRIER, p. 4; Hallestrandsfoto, p. 6; kavram, pp. 6-7; Andrey Shcherbukhin, p. 8; Yevhenii Chulovskyi, p. 9; Rudmer Zwerver, p. 10; Nenad Nedomacki, p. 11 (white-tailed eagle); Kevin Wells Photography, p. 11 (Atlantic salmon); JOHANLETANG, p. 11 (humpback whale); Pav-Pro Photography Ltd, p. 11 (reindeer); Kiev.Victor, p. 12; V. Belov, pp. 12-13; Rob Kints, p. 14; KatrineAanensen, p. 15; Samantha Scheel, p. 16 (waffles); Olga Miltsova, p. 16 (brunost); Katerina Poz, p. 16 (open-faced sandwiches); imageBROKER.com/ Alamy Stock Photo, p. 16 (rømmegrøt); Helen H. Richardson/ Contributor/ Getty Images, p. 17; fotografcic, pp. 18-19; Gonzales Photo/ Alamy Stock Photo, p. 20; Olena Tur, p. 21 (Bryggen); Marina J, p. 21 (Oslo Opera House); Frank Lambert, p. 21 (Vøringsfossen Waterfall); b113, p. 22.